Hyperion

Hyperion

Harry Matthews

Harry Art Publishing

First published in this edition December, 2020
by Harry Art Publishing
www.HarryArt.co.uk
England, U.K.

Typeset and designed in Venice by Harry Art Publishing.
Cover from original photographs 'Through the Needle's Eye: At The Wrekin'
& 'The Needle's Eye: Fire Altar and God's Covenant' by Harry Matthews
© Harry Matthews.
Cover design by Harry Matthews.

First Printing, 2020

A CIP catalogue record for this book is available from the British Library.

ISBN 978-1-8383498-1-3

In conformity with the expressed desire of the author, this volume is dedicated (by permission) to The Master
(& Thomas Bebbington, Esq.)
by his humble and obedient *serva*

The Publisher.

Epigraph I

Yet he no more, as yesterday,
Falls down into the sea;
What dost thou care, o shape of clay,
If it is I or he?

Mihai Eminescu, *The Vesper*, 1883.

Epigraph II

στῆσεν δ᾽ Ὑπερίονος ἀγλαὸς υἱὸς
ἵππους ὠκύποδας δηρὸν χρόνον, εἰσότε...

the bright Son of Hyperion stopped
his swift-footed horses a long while, until...

The Homeric Hymns, Hymn 28. 13-14.

Epigraph III

For me, dark, dark,
And painful vile oblivion seals my eyes:
I strive to search wherefore I am so sad,
Until a melancholy numbs my limbs;
And then upon the grass I sit, and moan,
Like one who once had wings.—O why should I
Feel curs'd and thwarted, when the liegeless air
Yields to my step aspirant? Why should I
Spurn the green turf as hateful to my feet?

John Keats, *Hyperion: A Fragment*, Book III. (1819)

Filled in, in pencil, in a transcript of Hyperion by Keats's friend Richard Woodhouse—

Glory dawn'd....

Contents

Contents

Contents

{ 1 }

Preface

This is the first edition of the third collection of my poems, that emerged in succession in August 2020, after the poems in the two months that formed the preceding collections. The poems in this collection are arranged as they were composed. They form a thematic whole arranged in sequence under the moniker *Hyperion*, alluding to the Greek etymology Ὑπερίων, which gives *hyper* & *aeon* (*above timelessness,* or *the high-one*).

I also chose the eponymous celestial being, *Hyperion*, being influenced by Hölderlin's epistolary novel.

Hyperion is about pondering the far-reaching changes that are upon us, and seeing our moral and spiritual outlook above time. *Hyerion* is a mighty genius, attracted to themes which portray the fate of those who bear the shock of the passage from one world to the next. Such a view opens up new poetic vistas of spiritual experience for readers. The fact that it may not at first sight appear clear, but that the very basis of our life may well be more profound than we have hitherto imagined; and that in the not too distant future we may see the urgent necessity for a complete re-evaluation of our ideas and the materialistic assumptions of our civilisation.

Hyperion helps us to see what we ordinarily are not conscious of. It is a collection of poems that has to be received creatively. Inevitably, the poetic thought and vision loses its divine perfection as it sinks into form: it can never have the beauty of its ideal, only a reflection. These poems are an attempt to feel into the urgent need for new ideas drawn out of the past, to create an expansion of thought and feeling for more harmony of human love in this world.

In the true spirit of concentrated creative power, *Hyprion* is a warning about the pitiful illusions in which we are in danger of being accustomed to, and that threaten a titanic struggle for our very existence. It is only through some drastic shock that we are able to leap beyond the narrow limits we can presently comprehend.

The poet passionately grasps the full import of what he can no longer ignore, and his vocation demands he permeates his work with his heart and idea. *Hyperion* stands eternally to express the agonising strife and hope, God willing, that we may be victorious in attaining a far higher level.

{ 2 }

The Great Physician

You drive in a heated frenzy without a goal...
You drive in the storm; you drive through country to the lake...

You crave the incredible

He grasps you...you long to be fulfilled.
He fills you...you shy away from the rest.

Alone with yourself,
Your worst enemy,
The solution is in the death:

Through Him,
Reproach dies.

{ 3 }

Hyperion

Why does this day have to be so hopeless?
Then you appeared, bare witness:[1]

As a brain bloated in a skull, like a super brain
Behind a dolphin's melon, a brain of two hemispheres:[2]
When one sleeps the other remains awake...

As a picture within which a man receives fire,
Your spirit is Holy, Eternal buoyancy;
You perceive Divine Holograms.

Who is your God? Desire all my certainties,
The True One is my archetype, above all others high.
Unmade by man, Lord of Mercy,
What the peace gave our taught muscles...
What has always gained us respect–
Fire and ice is our derivation of Inner Light:

There he is where my ignorance is lost.
Who was last riddle and answer to evil-loads?
Then new outbreaks surge through *noosphere*,[3]
False gods swell with stagnant airs,
And living dead pull down Fallen worlds.

The daemon is the secret of lowest circumstances,
Held forth as decisive. When it's condemned
With vapidity, the Enemy shows its futile range:
Son from the indigo generation[4]
Has died, resurrected in Central Sun.[5]

{ 4 }

Perplexing Legacy

Bright clearing dance to age you!
Dive gold-footed into purple lights.

So yields your frigid absolution;
Joy cries out through cracking shell.

I languish in years without you,
Such denial-exposure -though uncertain; our trial.

You never will bury that flawed fortune,
Your unsavoury agreements, squiffy sagas retold.

Enslaved, unconscious; full of shame yet acting shamelessly,
You speak in the wisest, most profane clarity when you say,

Who prides himself on such wanton abandon-
A modern, exhausted nest egg born in blood.

Hyperion

You hurl unspeakable abuse into the matrix of time,
A fast flowing, dark flood sweeps you– out of this lifetime...

{ 5 }

God's Hill

On distant crest, that rising Hill
A vision knitted to the Will
Of Yahweh, One I AM, stands as
Sentry of the Lord, the unseen
Presence

Accords with All He does in Love
– For love is God– and Light springing
Like the healing grasp of angel
Wings

As tree-arms wave in the cold breeze,
Swaying in a rainbow.

{ 6 }

Dark Fire

There was not much time was there? What fire!
As if you wanted to die to yourself anew,
Bright burning firework launched into the darkness...

The days with dancing in the sand dunes,
The fleshy pole and the white spray,
Wearing nothing...dark skin tone, melding, the sweat
And all agreement in the smiling, knowing kisses.

Then when it rose within us, invisibly a third,
I was obsessed with you; my brain squalled in throes,
Delighted you to swear to the heavenly city and to be anointed.
Until the very last you asked: *come, come, come,*

You hold your trumpet and blow in the great swirl
Of our dedication, sanctifying the death dance,

In our dark love, that dream as real as day!

The tent was filled with meek groanings,
Sparks sprayed in musty scents
Existing contradictions twitched
With proud clasp you display your ingenious prowess.

Your memory is like embers on driftwood fire
Dream that casually seeks to expand itself,
It gladdens me and became brighter...
So I sat enthralled in the moon circle with you...

Where is the cold dark fire,
The dirty water between us?

{ 7 }

You're Still Beginning

On your way down there- Lord of Chaos-
My price penetrates your star.

In the beginning there was little Light over our Shire,
The Church spire now a county museum
And the interior foreign glazed.

When tea light prayers to the Virgin mother sealed us up more loving of one another
Fasting with hope to St. Winifred an encounter: after the unhappy suitor.

The sacred depths reached by that once dim flickering flame
By an altar where the God man sacrificed all
In payment for the present redemption...

Then you came from your own kingdom

Striking as a rugged portrait and rough as a sordid dream,
In the naked touch of your infinite aspect towards me:

Since unfulfillment came from de-consecrated hands
Then it became dark and all desire was rapturous.

{ 8 }

You're Still End

You know who I am...only smell the
Sweat and cry for eternity at your shrine.

I did not begin with this taint, and the spirit your joy.
What makes me animal makes me human, now the end nears,
In which God will determine your new design.

I am unchanging, false, the wrong thing.
I'll be like you one lifetime: the choice was never made.
So bring the paper boats and flowers
And set them as river *pujas*[6] in memory of me.

{ 9 }

You're Still Middle

And past the impure purple flame: hello!
The leap is already taken to that broken end.
I have become what you wanted. You leave the union,
The rebirth that takes me from you who is most unlike me:

Your light that gives me wisdom and thankfulness,
Your life that is etched deep in my heart.

{ 10 }

Fate

The current flows down river,
There follows your wild heart
In which a fire burns across the incarnations.
It wants to spread its depth across time.

That life is heavily covered.

You cannot discharge the dark
– the reflection of your last life.
It weighs too heavily, after the shadows
You cannot be freed.

Perhaps now you know the price of bloodletting?

Poisons injected into your once endless, proud veins...
Till you surrendered your heart up to God,
Behind me, unbeknownst.

I cannot seize hold of you to pull back
Your body from that narrow divide.

The span barely includes one arm.
It releases all your troubling thoughts,
And exiles you into the night
You are fated for.

{ 11 }

Lumpenproletarian

You have certain desires for chavs.[7] Why is it that
After the modern world, they become hooded monks?
You composed yourself in conventional places.
Your cheap, gentle, matured mind emancipated,
Your foolish mix of the scag and booze; the vomit.
You leave off your leisure with reprobates– though you,
Dark-skinned and cold, are possessed: A god of your own,
A dragon chased to defeat by an Archangel,
A young man without a grey Adidas tracksuit.

{ 12 }

Creation

Holographic, every strong thunder
Exits from the sky and all the mud is swept.

Did they see your lightning on the horizon?
They are all foolish and cognisant of the unreal.
You expunge everything you use.

What could have been elevated from destruction?
He found you in the brightest appearance.
What an entrance..!

Thus, you rose powerful in the day,
Sparkling like a diamond around the fire of revival.

{ 13 }

Therefore boding

Go to the pool they say that is alive,
The murk of the dull banks just beside it,
The stained sky with the unusual smear,
Thick darkness breaths on the potent water.

The black, the burning shades seduce
Oak leaves, hawthorn bushes, biting is the wind.
Unhallowed, the retarded redwoods sway,
As spit and hiss disperse dusk that flattens...

Dark wind tosses, coiling vine foliage,
(Mulch stench and mushrooms that breed bondage)
Climbs in league on league of darkest verdure.

Within this solemn dream a bright snake stirs...

{ 14 }

Hortus Informal

Moon with a vibrant Spring
Acre of your hectares, trees
Straighten then the hall past the forest...

Up through the crack in the ground
Naked dancing on the lawn,
Tree branches are swaying,
Now the stars are shooting,
Memories of the loved one's spark in their minds.

Empty your pockets when you care to!
Clothes hung on the statues,
Flesh swept beneath the breezy willow,
Weeds gathered on the bonfire,
Strange orchids glare in the glass house!

In the yew maze, in the circle,

Hyperion

Enchanted, the sap is rising!
Disenchanted, a hare praying.
The air is moist on wet lettuce.

{ 15 }

After the Rain: Bow

The summer field is deluged with God's fire,
And from a midland field of wheat and poppies
I saw my friend run naked through the flames...
That glee of ever-nearing rainbow sheen untamed.

The evening after tranquil day is peace:
The spurned fields turned to a glorious sea,
And timely bright the colour wave in June,
The wide arched rainbow with its love *jejune*.

Then through sea of yellow-red you go
And brazen is the rainbow path you tread,
You bid us suck and join you in display
And yield: the peacock flaunting in the play...

Did I not see you in your stormy shade–
This crown of thorns, I never could have known

Hyperion

More than moon, in dark days, for me you shone,
And morning glory's less now you are gone.

{ 16 }

Delphic Pharmakon

Far overseas I went exiled, mean spirits
Had banished me...their darts ran through my heart
But in the sea sanctuary, waking strength profligates.

I saw the Isle temple's shrine beguiled,
And he, my Son, inherits my wreckage:
His mind still retreats from my bondage,
My distasteful thoughts run in his wild blood...

My life, savage starting, rises in candid joy,
But hell is relentless to punish my breach.
It wants blind men who can't escape the harpies.

I shall be fire, the midwife of dolphins,
That profane offspring seek to inherit.
Within their playful spirits lives
The hidden pearls of continuous wisdom.

Hyperion

The ocean breathes softly on dolphin skins.

I spoke the Word; the spiral has been freed...
With the Light fall, I shall be cured with ease,
To imagine belief: through cherished seas,
Unhindered, I leap on the remedies.

{ 17 }

Outlaw

All the Salopian lads flocked to you, in
A potent quest for horn powder and pipe.
You devil, how you lured more sons of darkness.

That conspiracy transpires to birth my lament.
I added the need of debauchery,
Persisted like a pagan, until I found God in you...

And only until this day do I fully comprehend
Your gifts, since I recall my own life as an outlaw:
Looking for you on the way, and at the riverbank.

{ 18 }

Profane

Those same lads that I harried in temptations
And starved and lowered me in need
Back then ineradicable disappointment: grief
That deep that I leave it in the painful night:

That I would throw your curses back
And in safer circles praise your foolish charms.
Everything that was said from the loud ones
And in the murmuration of smoke and groanings,
Profanes the revelation of your
Diabolical and sanctified mysteries...

{ 19 }

Auguries of Madness

This is the rarest experience that you enjoy,
Every time you rise, you endure to the end.

You are single, on the edge, and you bind the doubt.
With the flight of inaugural auguries, many drown.

The second, the best– swim and sink.
You held your head, yet you are so subdued around here,

That which breaks everyone does not break you:
If the weak open to the play of the crisis onset

Then you show the shallow one is doubtless...
Fortunate, soulful shift, you will be the first penitent.

{ 20 }

Outcome

When your youth announced your quest,
You were a rebel disregarding grave-eyed reproach
And endured many pains for one so young.

Then your star stirred, and you clamoured to come out
To ignorant villagers who could not understand you, yet
The questions came with such distasteful curiosity

Minds closed that no mouth could persuade, never heard...
They lured you along with fake acceptance, then pushed you down: LEAVE!
Such an uncertain path that closing, gains cowardice for you, desertion for them.

Of yourself, you cannot help what you are born as–
Do not weigh heavy with their condemnation nor apologise too much to them...

Be a level mountain to the plain, a river bending beside it.

{ 21 }

Online Quest

The Impossible happens in tadpole bursts,
Tenacity, and the questing sense of poets–
You follow the earliest dream in every work!

You made the quest out of the questions of the body,
Went as if misled, and you learned hard how to accept your-
self
When the *cybersphere* brought everything in view...

Dubious hyperlinks click deeper in littoral meanings,
After congratulations, you multiply praise with likes,
And calmly log into that distant virtual land.

{ 22 }

From Darkness to Light

Whoever put that darkness in you?
Knows that you must release yourself from curses
That you self-imposed, brought out to the bondage
Of parents, only works by the blood that spoils
The evil design that yearly sorrow gave away.

I want you to overcome darkness with Light,
To withdraw yourself from evil God enemies,
So I have to see how you will grasp Truth,
How can I be enclosed as you would have me?

A stranger unto myself, I do my shadow work
And join myself to the hope of future liberty.

{ 23 }

Fighter

Call it the starlight, that hit the glint in the captain's eye:
The thing that came into me at my coming...
It is tangible and shot like a fountain of cream.
Call it the flume that doesn't escape anything,
Call it a fore-fired thought-torpedo:

There are no aphorisms: as logic and reason
Are shibboleths to him. What he wants to represent?
I am not coming to suppress the tribulation needed for God's
    Kingdom:

For the sake of an evil arrow
I follow the name of God; I fight in the ring.

{ 24 }

The Glory Thief Comes When You Most Expect Him

Love came with the sex, from the start. That township.
The river called to the bard. The heat made him hard,
Also healed his heart, and that hurt,
His verse encouraged the breaking,
To bring the mending, and he arrived for a long time...

This is how Destiny likes scourging with a frown:
My God of escape, flesh sent to me in the gloom
To tempt me with bitter substitutes– those lithe, solid thighs,
The provocation of mighty lust's sultry, short-lived lies.

{ 25 }

Bipolar

Expedition to the pole,
I swing North to South in a nanosecond.
Biceped and homogeneous, the possessor, the possessed,
Full of *Eros* then *Agape*, fire then ice, all smoky,
As dragon burns monkey, as visionary is also fool,
As weapon is also a tool...

The wafer gives the waif Salvation,
From the priest who is a plebe;
And it melts on the hot coal tongue of fire.
There are criminals who become Saints,
Waste water can be purified, and the conformer
Was once a man who rebelled.

Up the pole or down it,
I am the beholder, and I am beheld,
But never the in-betweener.

{ 26 }

Ceremony of the Holy Fire

Free me from harsh words of evil men.
Because I do not care for worldly fools.
Let me rise above these narrow ghouls,
I am better than them by a factor of ten.

Here is what you can do, that is fight.
When I pray with you with the midnight oil,
I notice through fire that God despoils
Evil growths of Satan He wants to smite.

The blood of The Lamb is against Satan.
Open your mouth with your crying heart
Speak victory to crush the devil's dart,
You must take command in this Holy arson.

Hyperion

From life-giving crystal fountain waters,
He cleans the wound from all that's pus and pain.
His sword of fire gives you the strength to maim
Dark hands of devils and witch's slurs.

Now be *wise as dragon and peaceful as dove,*
Evil arrows of delay and madness
Backfire, return fast to the jealous,
They blaze returned on the flames of His love!

{ 27 }

Farewell

I observe the unmasked hypocrites: Godless
Enemies, full of pride, who deserve the lash.
Lord bless heroic suffering! I outwit their
Wicked arrows with the shield of God's wrath.

Then I am river borne on a coracle,
Struck by the Lord's enemies, on the current
Carried from that chaotic mess, dismal joy...

Lost vagabond, extend your arms into the
Night, the mockers say, you only follow them.
What thoughtless goad, and all the rest is
Drowning...amusement of the Great I AM.

{ 28 }

Desert Pagans

You call out the depleted, dark times
In your honest, wild absurdness:
They wanted to disable a camel with pus, a great abomination.

With an able sneer, bucolic triumph, and obstinate idolatry...
You are less clean than the last to infect the high altar.

Refusing to bow down to a family idol, in your stained homage,
Aiding such atrociousness; retarded obsequiousness,

Such indecency like in no generation before;
You thrust your vile worst up another foxhole.

You name it *endemic*, and you want to injure
Fighting in a wet skid risk, until you lick your lolly,

Brazen and lustful, violently in the devil's domain,
Satan's suppuration must be discharged; opened and drained.

{ 29 }

Run down the sea

Waves white streak the distant sea,
From grey faint mist and storm shadow,
Then a blood streak drips near here on the loud scar crag.

Be loud with me about the Supreme God:
Before I was redeemed why did I sit
Down for the silence, as the lukewarm do.

Cleanse me with hyssop for my milk and honey...
Heavy in safety, like honeycomb bees,
Losing your morning until the Queen came,

Afraid of harvest, your stores of pollen,
Adversaries busy with past extractions.
Your coming night is receding. Sweeteners,

Out of persuasion, lull you softly to sleep.

Now only one course remains: it is low tide,
Your modest genius of the calm sea shaved tomorrow.

You sail your latent fire with indignant crimson.
You only have fake ones for scrimmage,
Angels of poetical peace that were sent by the Maker.

You have the lion's look from God.
You banish timidity that tastes the fresh potential
Of everything that became an answer since you bled

That ink by which you outlive your exertions,
Wrestling every night for your
Star's return.

{ 30 }

Striving in the Path of God

You build invisible policemen to enforce restraint:
What is low can be lower! But you find
Running towards a stanchion in the dark...the edifice teeters.
And at the start of folly you raise hell:
What to do before we breathe in our own blood?

Before your own growing nose, your hate heart eats you out.
He cries too soon for action then antidote. Envoy of white-collar crime...
The profane sanity must strike as many as come against you,
God's wrath must strike ten thousand, yes,

His finger only will do
For the tens of thousands of *jihadis*.[8]

{ 31 }

Nothing Left to be Desired

You still finish us off in the end and for the start,
That you bind us with the relief of union,
You know who I am...just listen to this:
The flow down the river...there leads his mind,
Wild, full of memories again. What flames burn!

His hands all fire, each finger tipped with light.
Striving, I turn from the answerable love.
Now I'm groaning into wholeness with you.
Who is your Love? All I ever fancied and hoped for
Within myself...

{ 32 }

Beating the Country for the Blackguard

'Twas a wild goose chase, and I know not what
Moved me to run after it.

He came up
Like a wild cat and went straight at me and
The wild ducklings were out on the pool, and
The woods were full of song. Wild, Quixotic
Notions of sacrifice flooded his mood
Of dejection.

The other idea was
Absurd— too wild for serious regard.
Out there in the dark there was the wild one,
Beating a tattoo; impatient clawing.
A loaded rifle; and hark! There was no

Danger of discovery on his nearing,

For it was a wild night of wind and rain.

{ 33 }

Flowing Repose

Pleading the precious blood of Christ,
The spirit in all prayer, above

The impure body under the
Gold white light and crimson, pink rain...

Welcomes him to see more starkly
The short deliverance into

Day's salvation, that he cleanses
Himself yet denies his body.

You catch yourself with the semblance.
You are pious and discerning

When God moves in your life,
When your loved one finds repose.

{ 34 }

Your Clapping Echoes

As your implosion proved the crash of destiny
All the mountains clapped like an applause for you.
Since your fall, indistinct echoes carried
This as the most awesome thing that you could hear.

When the mountain announced your departure,
The impossible happened with premature
Delay to me who you gave your light to.
Call it the illumination of my eye
(Tyranny was our progenitor, as
Slavery was our prenatal cradle).

Comes silence before the splendour, comes
The Light across the fields. The wheat glowing,
I am one and the same with it, in peace,
From the golden glow in cloud dark anger
Having nothing, unaware they praise God,

Therewith, the eye of the Sun, who you call tame?

Your mind transformed by the centre without end.

{ 35 }

Selene

You must win me for the Light.
You must save me as the poor one.
You make me miserable.
Let's be calm! Give it harmony!
Otherwise I want to break you,
Otherwise lead you to perdition.
You should feel the Moonlight,
It will bind your enchantment.

{ 36 }

Medea

Sore eye of Pascal Moon excited her
Like the faint gleam in the fold of your shroud,
Before I perplex your paradise
And what you finished, incompetent,
No play of the nightmare could pull you,
Could barely freeze you still and confuse
Darkness that lies to you through her.

She is dark...If she ever rises from evil,
Do expose her succubus in the way of shadow,
Dullest phantom, where she invokes things
Cackling in her vile mirror!

{ 37 }

Climacus

Our day is dark, dry, and it punishes us
Into that drought where we thirst,
Amaurotic and glazed...don't you see?
Where she takes you without me?

When our eyes meet yours sparkle.
I am entranced by your outer form
And then you embrace me. Climbing higher
To you I blush, tightening my hold,
And stand upward towards you:

That is because I feel my own heat–
In near spaces between us, breathe
With your diffident, submissive end.

{ 38 }

To the Last Gasp

I should fill my line's end with my love's colour
If we are drawn like robin's to earth worms:
Where I give myself to you and only feel less,
The place we live complicates more and conceals...

You are fading and no one is blooming like me...
See this cloudy day fastens all misfortunes
To its clamouring, wretched, deformed back.
You misconstrue the truth to suit your lies.

You came to me from a terrible loss
After capricious injury as if I had hurt you.
I can fight you if you want to the last.
I hate you, like wanting nothing that lasts.
You are for me so long as the losing offers it.
My love is more like death than joy, misery,

The part of *Eros* that tortures my needs.
The opposing my wants brings you pleasure.

{ 39 }

Baffled

What happiness is provoked!
Affection is now indifferent.
And the devil only gives misunderstanding.
Tame reality sprouts fictions
Where you create yourself in me...
Now the lower poetry determines
How I lost myself in you.

{ 40 }

Maculate Muse

He who does not return his love is not worth it.
He who uses weakness to acquire others
Must laugh: who is rich who has not always gained...

You are the discouragement seeker whose
Level is revealed where dirty waters rise through
The plug hole, when pipes of gold rest in the cellar.

Do be afraid: why not me? Do throw me aside
Despite the expectation because you
Do understand but detest and hinder,
When curiosity insists you always question the *status quo*.
How do you change your colours so easily?

{ 41 }

Grope Passage

Knowing what I was searching for
Did you also know the poor man within me?
The tide that recedes near the island of chance,
The stuck desires in the sands of progress?

My wisdom is clipped clean by the cutlass of age.
I was fast asleep until the enemies came.
You only looked at my needs and scoffed,
Imprisoned me in your unreliable
Promises, so that you might go on living
In your death.

You have taken my gift as your greed dictates.
You do not speak until I toss the coin,
Provoking pain unless your pocket is satisfied:
You are the beggar who licks the wine cask in hope
That he may taste the dregs of the noble's wine.

Your grope down that passage betrays you.
I'm weary of your trouble, your pervasive storms,
So costly, you would throw yourself

Into the Void.

Footnotes

1. ^ Hyperion... Ὑπερίων, *Hyperíōn*, 'the high one', one of the twelve Titan children of Gaia (Earth) and Uranus (Sky) who, led by Cronus, overthrew their father Uranus and were themselves later overthrown by the Olympians. With his sister, the Titaness Theia, Hyperion fathered Helios (Sun), Selene (Moon) and Eos (Dawn).
   Hyperion's son Helios was referred to in early mythological writings as Helios Hyperion (Ἥλιος Ὑπερίων, "Sun High-one"). In Homer's Odyssey, Hesiod's Theogony, and the Homeric Hymn to Demeter, the Sun is once in each work called Hyperionides (Ὑπεριωνίδης, "son of Hyperion"), and Hesiod certainly imagines Hyperion as a separate being in other writings. In later Greek literature, Hyperion is always distinguished from Helios; the former was ascribed the characteristics of the "God of Watchfulness, Wisdom and the Light", while the latter became the physical incarnation of the Sun. Hyperion is an obscure figure in Greek culture and mythology, mainly appearing in lists of the twelve Titans:*Of Hyperion we are told that he was the first to under-*

stand, by diligent attention and observation, the movement of both the sun and the moon and the other stars, and the seasons as well, in that they are caused by these bodies, and to make these facts known to others; and that for this reason he was called the father of these bodies, since he had begotten, so to speak, the speculation about them and their nature— DiodorusSiculus (5.67.1)

2. ^ Bottlenose dolphins (Tursiops truncatus) have an absolute brain mass slightly greater than that of humans. Like humans they have two hemispheres. Dolphins sleep only one hemisphere of their brain at a time. The dolphin brain has a neural area devoted to visual imaging that is only about one-tenth that of the human brain, while the area devoted to acoustical imaging is about 10 times as large. Researchers in the USA and UK made this significant finding when they used a new piece of technology, a CymaScope, to translate a dolphin's clicking sounds into a holographic image of the submerged man the dolphin was echolocating.
3. ^ Noosphere, from the Greek νόος ("mind", "reason") and σφαῖρα ("sphere"); a sphere of evolutionary development of consciousness; mind &interpersonal relationships. As the Earth's "mental sheathe," the noosphere represents the breakthrough to a new consciousness, a new time and a new reality arising from the biospheric crisis. This is known as the biosphere-noosphere transi-

tion.Just as the biosphere is the unity of all of life and its support system, the noosphere is the unity of all mind and its thinking layers. In this way the noosphere can be understood as the sum of the mental interactions of all life. This perspective of the noosphere, as an evolutionary event, has been scientifically anticipated by Pierre Teilhard de Chardin, the noted French paleontologist, as well as his colleague (with whom he jointly coined the word noosphere in 1926), Russian geochemist, Vladimir Vernadsky (see The Theory and History of the Noosphere).

"The historic process is changing dramatically before our eyes ... Mankind taken as a whole is becoming a powerful geological force. Humanity's mind and work face the problem of reconstructing the biosphere in the interests of freely thinking mankind as a single entity. This new state of the world we are approaching without noticing it is the 'Noosphere.'" V.I. Vernadsky

The Internet is the third-dimensional reflection of the noosphere, a form of proto-telepathy. When the noosphere is fully activated, then the human species will experience telepathy as a collective norm.

See: José Argüelles , Foundation for The Law of Time.

4. Indigo Generation: *Who are believed to possess special, unusual, and sometimes supernatural traits or abilities*. Stenger, Victor J. "Reality Check: the en-

ergy fields of life". Committee for Skeptical Inquiry, 1998. Indigos are more empathetic and creative than their peers and have the colour indigo pre-eminent in their auras. [Tappe], Nancy Ann. *Understanding Your Life Thru Color: Metaphysical Concepts in Color and Aura.* Starling, 1986.

Descriptions of indigo children include that they:

- Are empathic, curious, and strong-willed
- Are often perceived by friends and family as being strange
- Possess a clear sense of self-definition and purpose
- Show a strong innate subconscious spirituality from early childhood (which, however, does not necessarily imply a direct interest in spiritual or religious areas)
- Have a strong feeling of entitlement, or deserving to be here

Other alleged traits include:

- High intelligence quotient
- Inherent intuitive ability
- Resistance to rigid, control-based paradigms of authority

Tober J & Carroll LA. *The Indigo Children*, Light Technology Publishing, 1999. According to Tober and Carroll, indigo children may function poorly in conventional schools due to their rejection of rigid authority, their being more clever or more spiritually mature than their teachers, and their lack of response to guilt-, fear- or manipulation-based discipline. Parents may prefer labelling their child an indigo as an alternative to a diagnosis that implies poor parenting, narcissistic parenting, damage, (Namka, Lynne (2005). "Selfishness And Narcissism in Family Relationships". *AngriesOut.com.* Archived from the original on October 1, 2002. or mental illness. (Carroll, RT (2009-02-23). "Indigo child". The Skeptic's Dictionary.). This is a belief echoed by academic psychologists. (Jayson, S (2005-05-31). "Indigo kids: Does the science fly?". *USA Today.*) Some mental health experts are concerned that labeling a disruptive child an "indigo" may delay proper diagnosis and treatment that could help the child or look into the parenting style that may be causing the behavior. Leland, J (2006-01-12). "Are They Here to Save the World?". *The New York Times.* Others have stated that many of the traits of indigo children could be more prosaically interpreted as simple unruliness and alertness.

5. ^ Central Sun. The Sun is at the centre of our Solar System and is the centre of Light, the intel-

ligence that governs this Solar System. The Sun is connected to every aspect of life and creates the world as we live in it. The Sun reads the vibrations and helps us to grow, if it feels our Love it feeds that Love, if it feels our fear it creates experiences for us to open up more fully to Love. The Sun is Light, and the Light allows us to see the mirror.The Sun is connected to the Central Suns. Our own Central Sun is Alcyone. The name Alcyone originates from Greek mythology; she is one of the seven daughters of Atlas and Pleione known as the Pleiades. Alcyone also means 'Kingfisher'.

The Sun is changing, its vibrations are heightening as we open up to the Sun within our Hearts. We are aligning also with the Central Sun as our journey back into alignment with the Sun is a cyclic completion. We are completing not only a 26,000-year cycle but also 500,000, and 2,000,000 year cycles as we return to our Source; back to God Creator.

6. The word *puja* is derived from the Dravidian *pu meaning* "flower". In its simplest form, a river *puja* usually consists of making an offering of flowers to Pagan gods in India. A River puja in England, for me, is a flower offering with a tea light candle, on a small paper boat decorated with flowers, set on a river as a prayer to God for someone who has died.

7. ^ "Chav", also "scally" in parts of England, is a British pejorative term used to describe an anti-social lower-class youth dressed in sportswear.
8. The first or the *classical* doctrine of *jihad* was developed towards the end of the 8th century. It emphasised the *jihad* of the sword (*jihad bil-saif*) rather than the *jihad* of the heart. In truth, the greater *Jihad* is of fighting evil within oneself.

Harry Matthews was born in rural Staffordshire, in 1980. After school in Shropshire, he read Philosophy and Politics at Reading University, graduating in 2002. In 2004 he wrote for the Amsterdam Weekly, after training in journalism, and pursued his passion for travel. In 2007 he started to write poetry, and in 2009 he started painting. He holds annual exhibitions of his paintings since 2012, and in the summer of 2020 wrote the poems that formed his first collections. He holds a Master of Arts in Writing from LJMU (2019).

Lightning Source UK Ltd.
Milton Keynes UK
UKHW010626100821
388609UK00001B/61